DRUM & BASS IS AN ELECTRONIC MUSIC GENRE CHARACTERISED BY ITS FAST-PACED BEATS AND INTRICATE RHYTHMS. EMERGING IN THE EARLY 1990S FROM THE UK RAVE SCENE, IT COMBINES ELEMENTS OF JUNGLE, BREAKBEAT AND TECHNO, AND HAS SINCE EVOLVED INTO A DIVERSE AND INFLUENTIAL GENRE.

AT ITS CORE, DRUM & BASS FEATURES A PROMINENT DRUM PATTERN WITH RAPID, SYNCOPATED BREAKBEATS, OFTEN ACCOMPANIED BY DEEP BASSLINES AND A VARIETY OF SYNTHESIZER SOUNDS. ADDITIONALLY, THE GENRE ENCOMPASSES VARIOUS SUBSTYLES, INCLUDING LIQUID, NEUROFUNK, JUMP-UP, AND MORE, EACH OFFERING UNIQUE SONIC CHARACTERISTICS AND MOODS.

DJS LIKE FABIO & GROOVERIDER, DJ HYPE AND JUMPIN' JACK FROST TOOK THE MUSIC ONTO THE LEGAL AIRWAVES OF KISS FM AND BBC RADIO 1, WHILST NIGHTCLUBS SUCH AS THE END AND FABRIC BECAME HOME TO WEEKLY DRUM & BASS RAVES. PEOPLE STARTED FLOCKING FROM ALL CORNERS OF THE GLOBE TO GET THEIR PIECE OF THE ACTION!

OVER THE YEARS, DRUM & BASS HAS EVOLVED AND EXPANDED, WITH ARTISTS CONTINUALLY PUSHING THE BOUNDARIES OF PRODUCTION TECHNIQUES AND SOUND DESIGN. TODAY, DRUM & BASS HAS A GLOBAL FOLLOWING AND REMAINS A STAPLE OF ELECTRONIC MUSIC FESTIVALS AND UNDERGROUND CLUB SCENES.

Words
Chris Dexta &
Alex Immerse

Editor
Colin Steven

Design
Banana Gun

Publishers
Southside Circulars
& Velocity Press

First edition
October 2023

southsidecirculars.com
velocitypress.uk

VP032

ISBN: 978-1-913231-45-3

THE ICON CATALOGUE
DRUM&BASS
VOL. 1

01. 31 RECORDS
02. AKO BEATZ
03. ARCHITECTURE
04. ASTROPHONICA
05. BASSBIN
06. COMMERCIAL SUICIDE
07. CREATIVE SOURCE
08. CRITICAL MUSIC
09. CYLON RECORDINGS
10. DARKESTRAL
11. DIFFRENT MUSIC
12. EXIT RECORDS
13. FLEXOUT AUDIO
14. FREAK RECORDINGS
15. HORIZONS
16. INGREDIENTS
17. INNERACTIVE MUSIC
18. METALHEADZ
19. MODERN URBAN JAZZ
20. NARRATIVES MUSIC
21. NONE60
22. PARADOX MUSIC
23. PENNY BLACK
24. PROTOTYPE
25. RENEGADE HARDWARE
26. REPERTOIRE
27. SAMURAI MUSIC
28. SCIENTIFIC WAX
29. SHOGUN AUDIO
30. SIGNATURE
31. SILENT FORCE
32. SOFA SOUND
33. SOUL:R
34. SUBTITLES
35. SYMMETRY RECORDINGS
36. PLAY:MUSIK
37. TRUE PLAYAZ
38. UVB-76
39. VALVE
40. WARM COMMUNICATIONS

31 RECORDS

1994 - PRESENT

Doc Scott's 31 Records is as seminal as they come. Always forward-thinking, with a catalogue spanning the full spectrum, and still going strong almost 30 years after its birth. Hard to pick just two essential cuts, the back catalogue is littered with them!

THE ESSENTIALS
NASTY HABITS 'SHADOWBOXING'
BUNGLE 'COCOONED'

AKO BEATZ

1996 - 1998 / 2014 - PRESENT

DJ Stretch's labour of love. After a small string of releases in the 90s, Stretch relaunched and it rapidly became a buy-on-sight cult label. A testing ground for the new talents, as well as established producers. Leans toward the more soulful breakbeat driven side of D&B.

THE ESSENTIALS
DOUBLE O 'DREAMING'
THRESHOLD 'BLACKBOARD EP'

ARCHITECTURE
1997 - PRESENT

Hard hitting, tribal beats are the order of the day for DJ Ink's Architecture. If you've been to a drum & bass rave in the last 20 years it's very likely you've nodded a head or tapped a toe to something from the back catalogue. Not for the faint-hearted!

THE ESSENTIALS
ARCHITEX VS LOXY 'SUBMERGED'
NOLIGE 'HUNTED'

ASTROPHONICA

2009 - PRESENT

Fracture & Neptune's lovechild. Initially home to their collaborations, but became known to host a wide range of experimental boundary-breaking releases, but still firmly rooted in the drum & bass blueprint.

THE ESSENTIALS
FRACTURE & NEPTUNE 'HULL BREACH'
FRACTURE 'BAD HABIT'

BASSBIN

2000 - 2007

Deep, dubby, and full of breaks. Ireland's Bassbin Records was on a roll from its first release in 2000. Releasing music from names like Alix Perez, Seba, Fracture & Neptune, and Breakage to name a few. These cuts will do serious damage on a big rig.

THE ESSENTIALS
BREAKAGE 'UNTITLED JUNGLE'
SEBA & PARADOX 'FROST'

COMMERCIAL SUICIDE

2001 - PRESENT

Klute started Commercial Suicide in 2001 with a string of energetic, dancefloor friendly 12"s and hasn't looked back since. There is something for everyone across the back catalogue, with silky Calibre cuts sitting alongside Amit's superb, moody debut album.

THE ESSENTIALS
KLUTE & MARCUS INTALEX 'MAKE A STAND'
AMIT 'SUICIDE BOMBER'

CREATIVE SOURCE

1995 - 2016

Run by one of the scene's original foundation DJs, Fabio. It leans toward jazzy-influenced beats but is still very much dancefloor focused. Some of the greatest D&B artists have passed through over the years!

THE ESSENTIALS
PRIMARY MOTIVE 'S'
LYNX 'DISCO DODO'

CRITICAL MUSIC

2002 - PRESENT

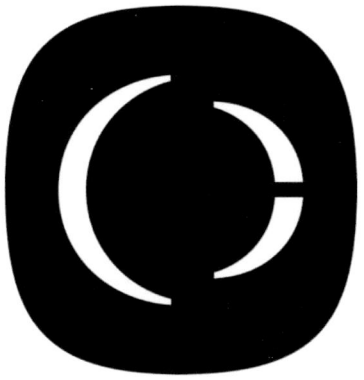

Headed by Kasra, who curates all types of drum & bass sounds for his label. The Ivy Lab EPs were instant classics and change hands for a pretty penny on Discogs, also home to Foreign Concept, Hyroglifics, Sam Binga amongst many others!

THE ESSENTIALS
CODE 3 'WHAT YOU SAYIN?'
IVY LAB 'AFTERTHOUGHT'

CYLON

2001 - PRESENT

Dark, moody D&B, of all styles!! Originally set up by Loxy & Dylan - this label has been a breeding ground for many artists in the more experimental realm. Cylon has always been one to watch, paving the way for others since the early 2000s.

THE ESSENTIALS
LOXY & RESOUND 'RAIN MAN'
LOXY & ISOTONE 'ANCIENTS (SKEPTICAL REMIX)'

DARKESTRAL
2007 - 2011

There were only ten releases on Darkestral but what it lacks in quantity, it makes up for in quality. Deep, dark and futuristic drum & bass for the heads. Instra:mental feature heavily on early releases with their cinematic soundscapes. Essential.

THE ESSENTIALS
INSTRA:MENTAL 'THE DEAD ZONE'
ROCKWELL 'REVERSE ENGINEERING'

DIFFRENT MUSIC

2010 - PRESENT

Known for its forward thinking and experimental drum & bass cuts, Diffrent Music has clocked up an impressive number of releases since it was formed in 2010. Even more impressive is the label's commitment to pushing up-and-coming underground artists.

THE ESSENTIALS
DEXTA & MAUOQ 'SLUGGER (TENSION DUB)'
FEARFUL 'TONGUES'

EXIT RECORDS

2003 - PRESENT

The sandbox for dBridge & his associates for the last twenty years. Artists like Skeptical, Mark System, Fixate amongst many others have built careers while releasing on Exit Records. Also guilty as charged for the whole Autonomic movement alongside Instra:mental!

THE ESSENTIALS
DBRIDGE 'FREEDOM CLUB'
DUB PHIZIX & SKEPTICAL (FEAT. STRATEGY) 'MARKA'

FLEXOUT AUDIO

2011 - PRESENT

Formed by Tom Bassi back in 2011, Flexout has been prolific with its release schedule, with over 180 releases at the time of writing! Plenty for any drum & bass raver to wrap their ears around, and no doubt plenty more to come.

THE ESSENTIALS
SURVEY & PRTCL 'PEOPLE IN SUITS'
ARKAIK '808 EP'

FREAK RECORDINGS

2003 - 2013

Hard edged label from Dylan, serving up a slice of B-Move horror style D&B for ten years, spawning several offshoots including Tech Freaks and Obscene - and more importantly, bringing people like Audio, Limewax, Current Value to the masses!

THE ESSENTIALS
SEBA & PARADOX 'PLANETS... STARS'
LIMEWAX 'UNTITLED 666'

HORIZONS

2005 - 2019

An early stomping ground for artists such as Alix Perez, Amoss, Data & Naibu. Also responsible for Inside Recordings and Progress LTD. All pushing the boundaries further than what was hot in the D&B world at the time.

THE ESSENTIALS
SEBA & PARADOX 'TIME STARTS NOW'
AMOSS 'GLURG MONSTER'

INGREDIENTS

2009 - 2017

Launched in 2009, by Clive (DJ Psylence) showcasing his love for the deeper side of the genre. Credited with helping bring through artists like Ruffhouse, Foreign Concept and Dead Man's Chest, the back catalogue blends the rough with the smooth to create a timeless blend of drum & bass!

THE ESSENTIALS
RUFFHOUSE 'THE FOOT'
SKEPTICAL 'COLD ONE'

INNERACTIVE

2002 - 2021

The late and great Spirit's (RIP) self-run label, heavily features his own productions, but is also home to music from Amit, Outrage and Marcus Intalex (RIP). Dark rollers and steppers for days!

THE ESSENTIALS
SPIRIT '20/20'
MARCUS INTALEX & SPIRIT 'ACID MONDAY'

METALHEADZ

1994 - PRESENT

The most recognisable label in D&B history. Formed by Goldie, Kemistry & Storm way back in 1994, 'Headz hit 100 releases in 2012 and is still going strong, with no sign of letting up. It's hard to put into words how much impact it has had not just on drum & bass, but underground music culture in the UK.

THE ESSENTIALS
AMIT 'GATECRASHER'
J MAJIK 'YOUR SOUND (SB81 REMIX)

MODERN URBAN JAZZ

1995 - 1197 / 2007 - PRESENT

Always exploring the more experimental side of drum & bass, Justice, of Moving Shadow fame, runs his own DIY label MJAZZ (pka Modern urban Jazz), which has redefined itself with every single release. Props to Metro's input over the years too!

THE ESSENTIALS
ICONS 'VERTIGO'
JUSTICE & METRO 'OXYMORON' LP

NARRATIVES
2012 - PRESENT

Atmospheric, original, deep. All adjectives that could be used to describe Blocks & Escher's Narratives Music. Dormant since 2020, but with the promise of more music on the way - quality over quantity is the ethos here. If you like something a little different, this is for you.

THE ESSENTIALS
ILK 'THE SOUND OF FALLING'
BLOCKS & ESCHER 'SAGAN'

NONE60

2011 - 2021

Blurring the lines between drum & bass and hip hop from day one, Hobzee & Zyon Base (aka Silent Dust) set up None60 to let off and facilitate a whole new world of experimental and half-time D&B, featuring Om Unit, Calibre, Dexta & Sinistarr.

THE ESSENTIALS
ETHOS 'REALITY'
SILENT DUST & SINISTARR 'THE CHANT'

PARADOX MUSIC
2003 - PRESENT

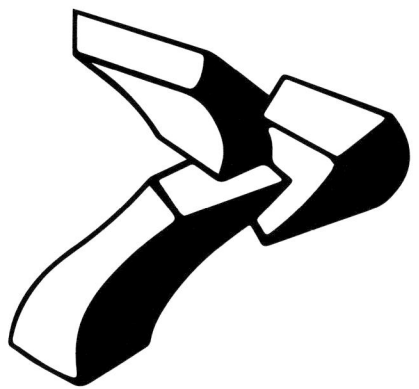

Dev Pandya (aka Paradox) has been a mainstay in the scene since his first release back in 1990 with DJ Trax as duo Mixrace! Famous for his intricate breakbeat manipulation and atmospheric samples, Dev's own productions dominate the back catalogue, with appearances from the likes of longtime collaborators Seba and DJ Trax.

THE ESSENTIALS
SEBA 'PIEMO FOR B'
PARADOX 'SOVIET'

PENNY BLACK
1996 - 2010

A subsidiary of Ray Keith's Dread Recordings, home to works by Twisted Anger, Serum and Special Branch (Threshold) - a mixed bag of atmospheric rollers and dancefloor destroyers!

THE ESSENTIALS
SERUM 'VILE'
TWISTED ANGER 'KINGCATCHAHOOK'

PLAY:MUSIK

2005 - 2010

Although there are only ten releases, there are some killer cuts to check out on DJ Flight's Play:Musik. Familiar names such as Martyn and Survival released early work on the label. Started in 2005 - a golden era of drum & bass.

THE ESSENTIALS
SURVIVAL 'STASIS'
MARTYN 'NXT 2 U'

PROTOTYPE

1994 - 2004 / 2017 - 2020

One of the most important D&B labels to ever grace a soundsytem! Grooverider's stronghold, featuring Dillinja, Ed Rush, Optical, Lemon D, Trace, Matrix, DJ SS - the who's who of the formative years of drum & bass!

THE ESSENTIALS
MATRIX 'MUTE 98'
ED RUSH, OPTICAL & FIERCE 'ALIEN GIRL'

RENEGADE HARDWARE

1996 - 2017

The institution! Hard-edged, techstep, d&b music on a big scale, Clayton & Mark brought through too many artists to mention, This was one of the biggest and baddest labels in the scene, with huge multi-arena parties and numerous sub-labels.

THE ESSENTIALS
USUAL SUSPECTS 'HOLE PUNCH'
KONFLICT 'MESSIAH'

REPERTOIRE

2009 - PRESENT

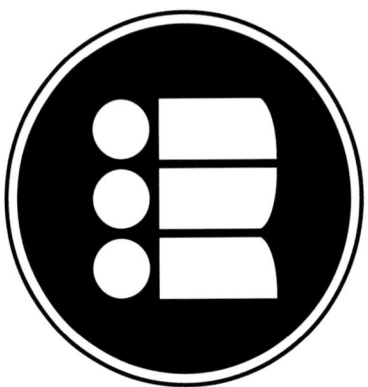

Modern day d&b / jungle imprint from Law, Ben, Wheeler, Kola Nut & RUNDR - showcasing a mix of cutting-edge sounds, a nod to the past and some more soulful rollers. Recently set up imprints R:Whites & Safe:Raver to fill in the gaps with other tempos!

THE ESSENTIALS
TIM REAPER 'LANTERNS'
ARTILECT 'SOMETHING ELSE EP'

SAMURAI MUSIC

2007 - PRESENT

Originally hailing from New Zealand, DJ Presha's label which originally focused on the more techy / rolling D&B, pivoted around 2013 and heavily moved to the more halftime, dark techno and breakbeat-influenced Drum & Bass.

THE ESSENTIALS
CLARITY 'BLUE RUIN'
HOMEMADE WEAPONS 'MIND CONTROL'

SCIENTIFIC WAX

1994 / 2005 - PRESENT

Breakbeat lovers, this is for you! Scientific Wax was originally launched in 1994 but only got as far as one release. It relaunched in 2005 and has been releasing killer 12"s ever since. Run by Sterling Styles (aka Equinox), and famous for its Amen breakbeat rollouts!

THE ESSENTIALS
BREAKAGE 'FORGOT THE NAME'
NOLIGE 'EYES DECIEVED'

SHOGUN AUDIO

2004 - PRESENT

Shogun is a label that has covered the full spectrum of drum & bass since its inception in 2004. Racking up a huge number of releases, the quality control has remained as you would expect from owner DJ Friction. Get stuck in.

THE ESSENTIALS
SPECTRASOUL 'ABSENTIS'
ALIX PEREZ '1984' LP

SIGNATURE

2003 - PRESENT

Self-release imprint from Belfast-born
Dominic Martin, aka Calibre. A mainstay
for the soulful, liquid drum & bass scene,
prolific in releasing 18 albums, many singles
and EPs in little over 20 years!

THE ESSENTIALS
CALIBRE 'YOU COULD DANCE'
CALIBRE & HIGH CONTRAST 'MR MAJESTIC'

SILENT FORCE

2014 - PRESENT

Silent Force prides itself on 'looking forward by looking back'. Focussing on releasing music from new and emerging producers - but always with a nod to the classic Drum & Bass / Jungle sound. Future thinking junglism!

THE ESSENTIALS
CHAOS SPY 'SCANNERS'
SICKNOTE 'INSIDE VIEW'

SOFA SOUND

2017 - PRESENT

Bristolian DLR has been on a mission over the last five or so years to bring you music that keeps the dancefloor bubbling while keeping it groovy! Sofa Sounds is only in its infancy but already made a mark!

THE ESSENTIALS
M-ZINE 'GEST'
ZERO T 'THE UNDERGROUND EP'

SOUL:R
2001 - 2018

Legendary imprint from the late, great Marcus Intalex. Launched in 2001, early releases from Marcus, alongside ST Files and Calibre, set the tone for what would become one of the most well-respected labels in the game. Buy on sight business! Rest in peace, Marcus.

THE ESSENTIALS
CALIBRE 'FIRE AND WATER'
VARIOUS 'DAT MUSIC VOL.1'

SUBTITLES

2000 - 2020

Norway's TeeBee has been releasing records since 1996, and in 2000 decided the time was right to launch his own imprint. On the techier side of the Drum & Bass sound, the label contributed to the rise of artists such as Noisia and Phace, alongside TeeBee's own productions.

THE ESSENTIALS
BREAK 'SUBMERGED'
FRACTURE & MARK SYSTEM - YEAH, BUT...

SYMMETRY
2006 - PRESENT

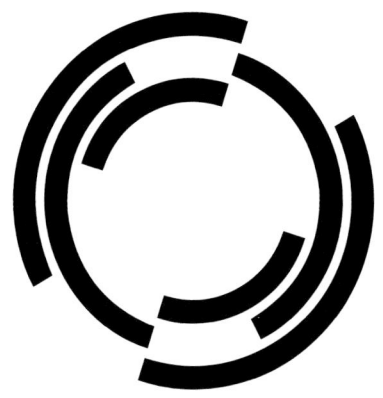

One of the drum & bass scene's favourite artists Break - releasing his own music and a select few fellow artists. Known for dancefloor based d&b in many flavours, Symmetry looks like the only way is up!

THE ESSENTIALS
BREAK & DIE 'SLOW DOWN'
BREAK 'SYMMETRY' LP

TRUE PLAYAZ

1996 - 2005

DJ Hype, Zinc and Pascal, aka the Ganja Kru, launched True Playaz in the dawn of the d&b realm, bouncey basslines, heavy beats and breaks aimed more on the jump-up edge, notably responsible for the rise of DJ Hazard.

THE ESSENTIALS
BROCKIE & ED SOLO 'MARS'
DJ ZINC 'REACH OUT'

UVB-76 MUSIC

2015 - PRESENT

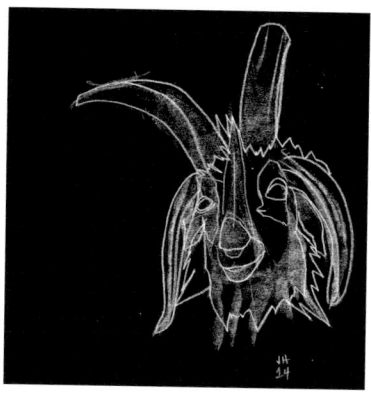

A link between Canada and Bristol, run by Gremlinz and Nick Vega, this experimental melting pot of techno & drone influenced drum & bass took the world by storm, Pessimist, Overlook and Clarity are the mainstays, and Droogs is the tooled-up sub-label

THE ESSENTIALS
MANTRA 'MINDGAMES'
PESSIMIST 'WPN-1'

VALVE

1997 - 2012 / 2020

Drum & Bass royalty Dillinja & Lemon D joined forces, set up a studio and label in Woolwich back in the late 90s and then destroyed dancefloors all over the globe! Bass heavy, big bad beats!

THE ESSENTIALS
CYBOTRON 'NASTY WAYS'
DILLINJA 'ACID TRACK'

WARM COMMUNICATIONS

2002 - PRESENT

Originally started stateside by DJ, EHL and sold to Triple Vison in 2019, Warm Communications has clocked up an impressive back catalogue of releases. Heavy hitters like Seba, Spirit (RIP) and Mark System all appear. Deep and dark sounds dominate alongside dancefloor friendly cuts.

THE ESSENTIALS
FRACTURE 'TUNNEL TRACK'
ILK 'THE HEATHER'

SOUTHSIDECIRCULARS.COM